Written by Gaud Morel
Illustrated by Sylvaine Pérols

Specialist Adviser:
U.S. Forest Service

ISBN 0-944589-43-X
First U.S. Publication 1993 by
Young Discovery Library
217 Main St. • Ossining, NY 10562

YOUNG DISCOVERY LIBRARY

Nature's Timekeeper—
The Tree

YOUNG DISCOVERY LIBRARY

Can you imagine a world without trees?

Surely no. Trees are everywhere, except the driest deserts and highest mountains. Trees grow even in the middle of cities, dressing up streets and plazas.

You know a forest (1) where trees
grow closely together. On the
sides of roads and rivers, trees are
planted in line (2). Fruit trees
grow in an orchard (3). Hedges are
small trees (4) or bushes (5)
planted to form a fence. A weeping
willow grows in this yard (6). Nearby
is a field of young fir trees (7).

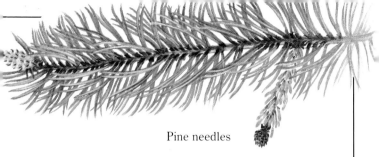

Pine needles

Trees are the biggest plants in the world

They can grow very tall... and very old. Unlike you and me, they keep growing all their lives! Their roots reach down, holding them firmly in the ground.

Oak leaves

Do you know what an oak tree looks like?

Its leaves are wide and flat, like your hand: it is a **broadleaf** tree. The leaves are shed in the fall. Pine trees have leaves like needles and keep them all year long. Pines are **conifers.** Coniferous trees, and bushes, are usually called evergreens. They grow cones and have a sticky sap called **resin**... used to make medicine and varnish.

A tree does not move or make noise, but it is alive!

A tree needs food and water just as we do. It takes them from the earth. The food and water, called **sap**, moves through tiny pipes the

Sap travels from the roots to the leaves.

way blood moves through your body. Trees use the sun to make oxygen for the air we breathe.

The sap moves in the veins of the leaves.

Leaves give off water. That is why it always feels cool and damp in the forest!

Roots reach deep into the ground to find food and water for the tree.

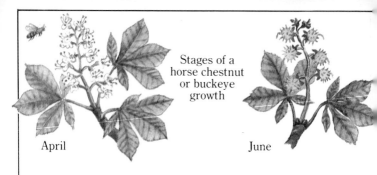

Stages of a
horse chestnut
or buckeye
growth

April

June

From flowers to chestnuts

May is chestnut blossom time.
The flowers smell good and bees
love this smell! They buzz in
and out, getting powdery **pollen**
all over themselves. Bees also
drop pollen. It gets on the tiny
pin, or pistil, in the middle of
a flower. Bees **pollenize** flowers.
The flower soon fades, but some-
thing new is growing. The pistil
is turning into a chestnut!

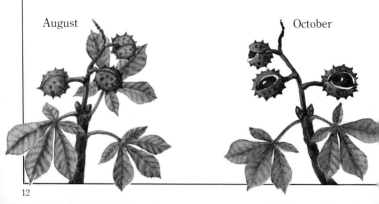

August

October

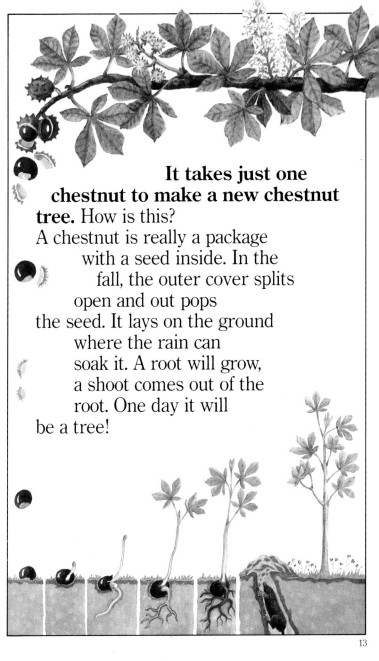

It takes just one chestnut to make a new chestnut tree. How is this? A chestnut is really a package with a seed inside. In the fall, the outer cover splits open and out pops the seed. It lays on the ground where the rain can soak it. A root will grow, a shoot comes out of the root. One day it will be a tree!

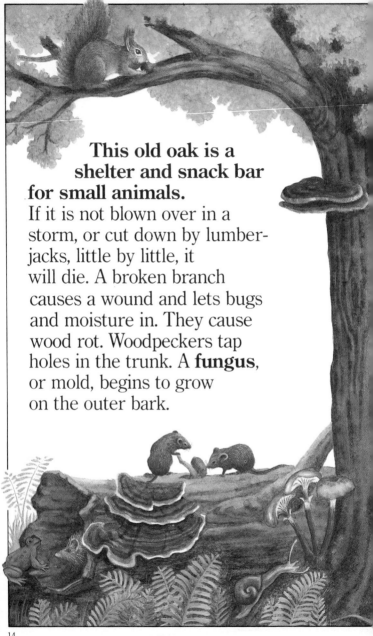

This old oak is a shelter and snack bar for small animals.
If it is not blown over in a storm, or cut down by lumberjacks, little by little, it will die. A broken branch causes a wound and lets bugs and moisture in. They cause wood rot. Woodpeckers tap holes in the trunk. A **fungus**, or mold, begins to grow on the outer bark.

Where do birds build their nests? Among the branches. What munches on the leaves? Caterpillars.

And squirrels—they eat the acorns.

Look at that hollow log. Centipedes and termites live inside and underneath. Snails and slugs make slimy trails over it.

One day the log will become part of the forest's rich soil.

In May, the leaves of the oak tree are bright green. They make a tender, tasty meal for caterpillars.

All trees make flowers.

2. Inside the buds, the new leaves are ready to unfold. They have been waiting for months— new life!

1. The trees have been dormant, asleep, during the cold winter.

Now the April sun warms them and wakes them. Spring is here.

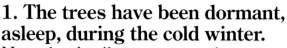

Some flowers have no petals; they are called catkins.

3. The flowers bloom. Have you ever seen oak flowers?

4. Oak trees make two kinds of flowers. The little balls turn into acorns, but they will need pollen from the catkins to do it.

It feels good to sit under a tree on a hot summer day!

It is always cool and shady there.

Leaves come in many different shapes and sizes.

3. These balls are galls. A gall wasp lays eggs on a leaf so the larvae can hatch and eat. The tree grows these hard bubbles to protect itself.

1. Insects buzz in the hot summer air. All the leaves are out and fruit is slowly ripening.

Leaves can be long, rounded, pointed...

2. The leaves of each tree can feed thousands of insects.

4. Aphids are tiny pests that suck sap out of the leaves. Ladybugs eat aphids and help stop damage.

19

In October, oak leaves turn red or brown.

All trees make fruit, even if some aren't good to eat.

3. Where are the seeds?
Inside the fruit. Some fruits break open. Then the wind carries the seeds away.

This squirrel is picking seeds out of a pine cone.

1. Autumn brings cool, crisp days. The leaves change to many colors. The leaves begin to fall with the first puffs of wind.

The seeds are now well-protected inside the ripe fruit of autumn.

2. The leaves fall but tiny buds remain, ready for the spring.

4. Mice and squirrels now gather and hide acorns and nuts for the winter. But they leave many that will grow into trees!

Winter is the best season to study the shape of trees.

Make a drawing of some trees in winter. Take special note of how the branches are placed.

3. By the time winter arrives, a tree already has all its leaves and flowers for next year. They are hidden inside the buds.

1. Everything is quieter in the winter, even the birds.
Insects hide under the fallen leaves. The trees rest.

2. Many broadleaf trees like holly (1), olive (3), and holm oak (4) stay green all year. Mistletoe (2) is a plant that grows on trees.

4. How are they kept safe from the cold and rain? Buds have a winter coat of sticky scales.

Peel a bud and you'll see young leaves or a closed-up flower.

Which trees grow in the mountains?

Mostly the conifers or evergreens. You will find each kind growing in its special place. The larch lives high up and likes a lot of sun.

larch

Firs like rain and fog. You'll see them on chilly northern slopes.

fir

Spruces are not fussy and will grow in sun or shade. They are very popular for use as Christmas trees.

spruce

Scotch pines are native to Britain but grow any-where it is not too hot. Squirrels like their tiny pine cones.

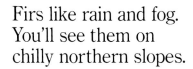
Scotch pine

Fast and slow growers

Mountain firs and poplars near water grow very quickly. Oak trees take their time. A fifty year-old poplar is as tall as a 100 year-old oak.

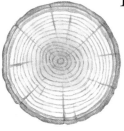

Count the number of circles in the trunk to learn the tree's age.

A ring for each year

Wood has dark and light rings. Each year a new ring is formed around the trunk, just under the bark. Widely spaced rings show fast growth. Close rings mean slower growth.

The tree is protected by its skin, the **bark**. If there is a hole in the bark, insects or a fungus can attack the tree. So, please don't nail a sign to a tree or carve your initials in the bark.

If you want to know the age of these fir trees, count the branches from the bottom up.

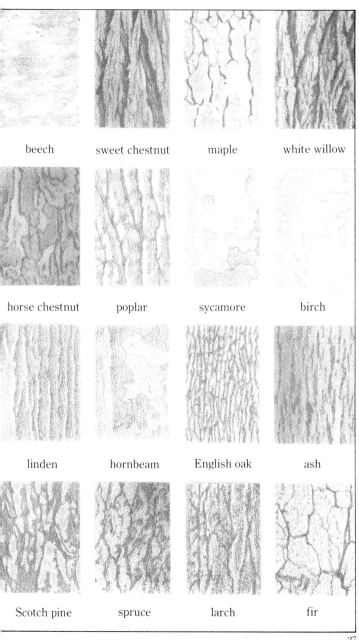

beech	sweet chestnut	maple	white willow
horse chestnut	poplar	sycamore	birch
linden	hornbeam	English oak	ash
Scotch pine	spruce	larch	fir

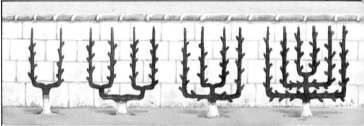

1. The pears and apples you eat come from fruit orchards or farms. The trees need special care.

Bushes and conifers are sold in pots, or with earth around their roots. Broadleafs can be bare.

3. Trees are grown in **nurseries** until they are large enough to be sold and replanted elsewhere.

2. The farmer carefully trims the branches. Chemicals are sprayed to protect the trees from disease.

Tools for the farm, nursery or garden: 1. hoe
2. rake 3. spade 4. trimming shears 5. sprayer...

4. The nursery worker will tell you the best time to plant your tree.

1. City trees don't have a lot of room to spread out! In the winter a **pruner** comes to trim them.

chainsaw

billhook

3. In the forest, lumberjacks are cutting full-grown oak trees.

2. Heavy trimming may be necessary because the branches can interfere with trucks or wires. This is not always best for the tree. Extra care must be used.

4. They then plant **seedlings** to replace the trees they have taken.

tree paint for cuts

pruning saw

Trees come in all sizes.
They are the tallest living
plants. But Arctic dwarf
willows are only a few inches
high. In Japan people grow
miniature **bonsai** trees in
their homes.

**The sequoia and redwoods of
California are giants.**
They average 300 feet—as
high as a 30-story building!

This olive tree
is over 1,000
years old.

Baobab trees live
only in Africa.

The trees with the thickest trunks grow in Mexico. They are bald-cypress trees. It takes 25 people, holding hands, to get around the trunk.

How old are the oldest trees? 4,900 years!
They live in the California mountains and are called bristle-cone pines.
Hot places cause odd shapes: look at the baobab and mangrove.

Sequoias are the world's largest trees.

baobab

The roots of mangrove trees are underwater.

The beech lives in cool forests and mountains.

The hornbeam is used for firewood.

Sweet chestnuts are grown for their wood and nuts.

Linden flowers are dried to make herb tea.

Ash likes moist soil.

Wild cherry fruit is sour.

Willow branches can be woven to make baskets.

Like a helicopter, maple fruit spins as it falls.

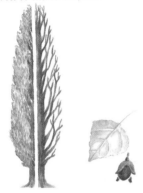

Soft poplar wood is used to make matchsticks.

Birch trees grow best in sunny clearings.

Horse chestnuts give beauty.

Planes do well in cities.

Best of All

Trees are short
and trees are tall,
and some grow leaves
to scuff in fall.

Trees are fat
and trees are thin
with windows where
the sun looks in.

Trees are big
and trees are small—
but **Christmas** trees
are best of all.

Aileen Fisher

(Reprinted
with Permission)

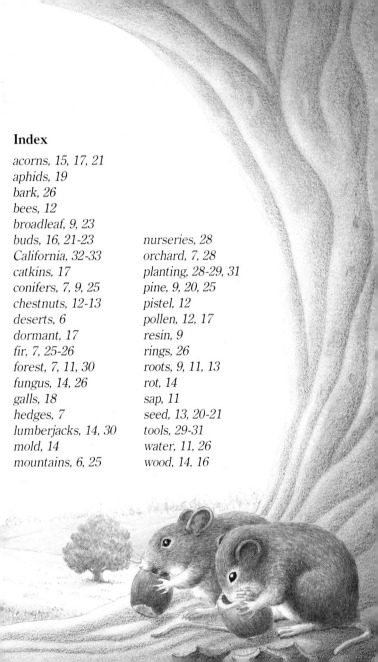

Index